# A Yak at the Picnic

Written by Roderick Hunt
Illustrated by Nick Schon,
based on the original characters
created by Roderick Hunt and Alex Brychta

OXFORD
UNIVERSITY PRESS

**Read these words**

yum          yak

neck         Jack

back         cups

tubs         bull

Mum set up the picnic.

An odd animal ran up.

It was a yak.

Mum put lids back on the tubs.

The yak was lost.

A man ran up.

It was his lost yak.

The man got Jack the yak
back.

## Talk about the story

# Word search

What words can you find with *k*, *ck* or *y* in them?

Can you write them down?

| a | k | i | m | t |
|---|---|---|---|---|
| s | o | c | k | s |
| o | d | e | c | k |
| y | u | m | f | d |
| r | p | a | c | k |

## Missing letters

Choose the letters to make a word

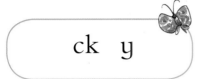

ck   y

_ak

Ja_

ba_

# A Man in the Mud

Written by Roderick Hunt
Illustrated by Nick Schon,
based on the original characters
created by Roderick Hunt and Alex Brychta

OXFORD
UNIVERSITY PRESS

## Read these words

mud

moss

fun

will

deck

mess

zap

jet

18

Gran had mud on her deck.

Gran had moss on the deck.

Gran had to get rid of it.

She got a jet.

The jet will zap it.

The jet was fun.

# Gran did a dog.

Gran did a man.

26

## Talk about the story

There was mud on Gran's deck. What else was there?

Why did Gran like using the jet?

What did Gran draw on the deck?

What would you have drawn on the deck?

## Missing letters

Choose the letters to make a word:

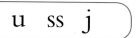

u  ss  j

f_n

_et

me__

m_d

fu_

# What's in the picture?

Match the words to things you can find in the picture. Point
to the ones you can find.

# Dad mud dog mess cat Mum jet

# Spot the difference

Find the five differences in the two pictures.